The Comp
Saxophone
Player

For E♭ Alto Saxophone

Wise Publications
part of The Music Sales Group
London/New York/Paris/Sydney/Copenhagen/Berlin/Madrid/Tokyo

Published by:
Wise Publications
14-15 Berners Street, London W1T 3LJ, UK.

Exclusive Distributors:
Music Sales Limited
Distribution Centre, Newmarket Road, Bury St Edmunds,
Suffolk IP33 3YB, England.
Music Sales Pty Limited
120 Rothschild Avenue, Rosebery, NSW 2018, Australia.

Order No. AM969738
ISBN 0-7119-8777-7

Cover and book design by Chloë Alexander.
Printed in the EU.

CD recorded, mixed and mastered by John Rose and Jonas Persson.
Music processed by Paul Ewers.
Instrumental solos by Ned Bennett.
Backing tracks by Guy Dagul and Paul Honey.
Edited by Heather Slater.

Your Guarantee of Quality
As publishers, we strive to produce every book to the highest
commercial standards. The music has been freshly engraved and
the book has been carefully designed to minimise awkward page
turns and to make playing from it a real pleasure.

Particular care has been given to specifying acid-free, neutral-sized
paper made from pulps which have not been elemental chlorine
bleached. This pulp is from farmed sustainable forests and was
produced with special regard for the environment.

Throughout, the printing and binding have been planned to ensure
a sturdy, attractive publication which should give years of
enjoyment. If your copy fails to meet our high standards, please
inform us and we will gladly replace it.

www.musicsales.com

Contents

About This Book

WELCOME TO THE COMPLETE SAXOPHONE PLAYER.

This revised and fully updated edition features the best of the four-volume course by Raphael Ravenscroft, with easy-to-follow instructions and photo demonstrations, and a wide range of music, from popular songs to light classics.

This book will guide you all the way to becoming a proficient player, starting with the very first time you pick up your instrument. You'll start to play right away, learning basic concepts through short excerpts from familiar songs. Soon you'll be playing longer selections, and eventually full songs.

There are two CDs with this book. Watch for the symbols and

The CDs include demonstrations of the exercises, plus full performances of the songs. You can also hear the backing tracks without the solo part, so when you're ready, you can play along.

No previous knowledge of the saxophone is required to use this book – from the very first session, you'll begin to experience the fun and enjoyment of making music.

About The Saxophone

The alto saxophone can be found in almost every jazz, marching band and concert band, and even occasionally in the symphony orchestra.

The saxophone was patented by the Belgian inventor Adolphe Sax in 1846. It is classed as a woodwind instrument because it uses a wooden reed.

Sax created the instrument as a link between the brass and woodwind families – although it is made of brass, its keys are like those of a woodwind instrument, and its mouthpiece and reed are very similar to the clarinet.

There were originally fourteen different types of saxophone!

Today, there are four models in common use:

The E-flat alto saxophone
The B-flat soprano saxophone
The B-flat tenor saxophone
The E-flat baritone saxophone

Parts Of The Alto Saxophone

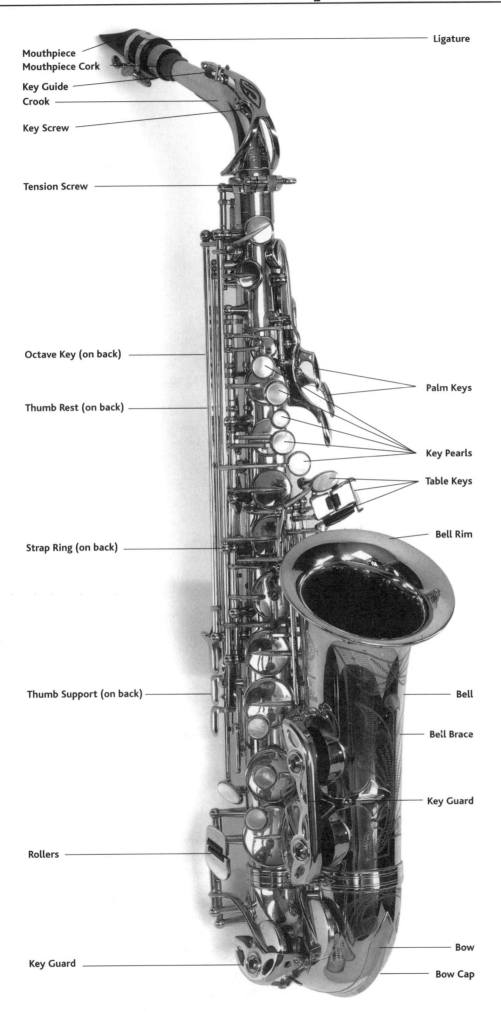

Mouthpiece
Mouthpiece Cork
Key Guide
Crook
Key Screw

Tension Screw

Octave Key (on back)

Thumb Rest (on back)

Strap Ring (on back)

Thumb Support (on back)

Rollers

Key Guard

Ligature

Palm Keys

Key Pearls

Table Keys

Bell Rim

Bell

Bell Brace

Key Guard

Bow

Bow Cap

Getting To Know Your Saxophone

WHEN YOU'RE READY to take your saxophone out of the case for the first time, follow these step-by-step instructions (follow these ten steps in reverse when you are disassembling your instrument).

• Cork grease

CORK GREASE

• A sling, or neck strap (this will have a hook at one end)

• The main body of the saxophone

• The crook (with cork around one end)

• Reeds (medium soft, strength 2)

• The ligature (this holds the reed against the mouthpiece)

• A crook swab (not shown) and a pull-through swab (below)

A 30 A

ALTO Saxophone
+ BASS Clarinet
+ BASS Flute

• Mouthpiece cap

• Mouthpiece

Step 1 Taking the saxophone out of its case

Your case should contain everything shown on page 6. Before you go any further, make sure you have everything listed.

Step 2 Checking and moistening the reed

Take one reed from the box. Examine it closely, making sure that it has no cracks or chips.

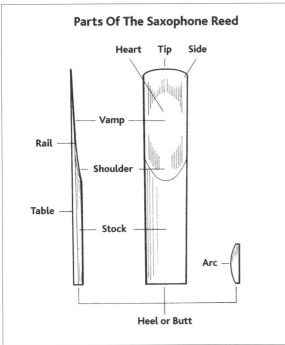

Parts Of The Saxophone Reed

Heart   Tip   Side

Vamp

Rail

Shoulder

Table

Stock

Arc

Heel or Butt

> ### TIP
> *Always handle the reed by its base –
> never handle it from the thin end,
> which can break very easily.*

Now, place one end of the reed into your mouth, and soak it with saliva.

Then do the same with the other end.

Another way to moisten your reed is to soak it in a small glass of water for a few minutes. This is a good idea if your reed is brand new, or if it hasn't been used for a while and is especially dry.

Otherwise, moistening the reed in your mouth is usually adequate.

No two reeds are exactly the same, even if they are of the same strength and come from the same box.

You'll find some reeds easier to 'play' than others – generally, if a reed is too hard, uneven, or thick, you might find it harder to make a sound when you are first learning to play.

To make a reed easier to play, check the underside – if it isn't perfectly flat, you can gently sand the bottom to make it more even.

Step 3 Preparing the mouthpiece

With the reed still in your mouth, remove the cap from the mouthpiece and loosen the screws on the side of the ligature.

Remove the ligature from the mouthpiece.

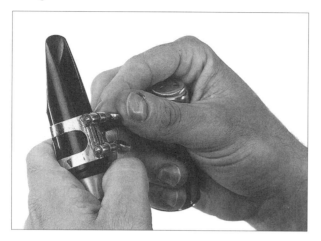

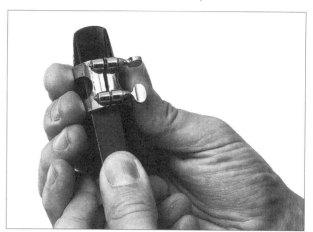

Step 4 Placing the reed

Gently place the reed on the mouthpiece, flat surface down, with the thinnest part against the tip of the mouthpiece.

Be careful of the reed's delicate tip, and check that it is exactly in line with the tip of the mouthpiece.

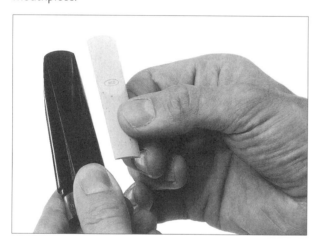

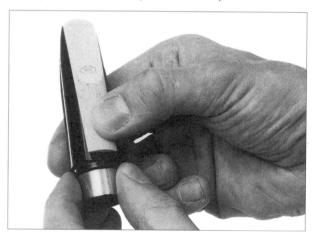

Step 5 Securing the reed

Put the ligature back over the reed until all three components (ligature, reed and mouthpiece) are in position.

Now tighten the ligature screws.

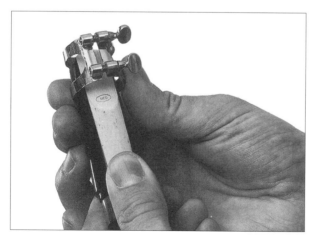

Replace the mouthpiece cover and return the complete unit to your saxophone case.
Before you play, always make sure that the reed is still in the correct position.

Step 6 Connecting the mouthpiece to the crook

Take the crook from the case and coat the cork with cork grease. Cork grease should be applied to the crook only when the mouthpiece will not slide onto it easily (once each week with regular playing).

Take the completed mouthpiece unit from your case and place it onto the crook.

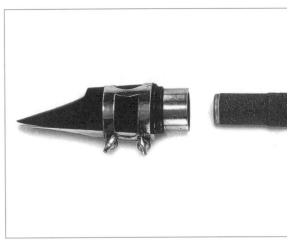

Gently twist it from side to side until it covers roughly half the cork. Put the mouthpiece and crook back into your case.

Step 7 Connecting the crook to the main body

Placing your right hand in the bell, pick up the main body of the saxophone and rest it against the bottom of the case in an upright position.

If you have an end stopper, remove it and then loosen the tension screw.

Listen for the soft click indicating that the crook is firmly seated. Adjust the crook, and tighten the tension screw.

Pick up the crook and mouthpiece unit, and gently but firmly insert the open end of the crook into the top of the saxophone.

TIP

Always keep the mouthpiece cover in your pocket while playing, and replace it as soon as you finish, even if you are only taking a short break.

The majority of reed accidents are caused by careless handling either before or after playing.

Step 8 Connecting the sling

Look at the back of the main body of the saxophone. About halfway down you will find a small ring. Connect the sling hook to this ring.

Now lift the whole saxophone out of the case and allow the sling to take the full weight of the instrument.

Step 9 Holding your saxophone

Halfway between the ring and the bottom of the saxophone, you will see a thumb support – this is for your right-hand thumb.

Above the ring you will find a thumb rest for your left-hand thumb.

With your hands in this position, gently grasp the main body of the instrument and bring it into the upright position. Your neck should take most of the weight.

Step 10 Adjusting the sling

Adjust the sling so that the mouthpiece is level with your mouth. With your head up and shoulders relaxed, let the saxophone come towards you.

Left thumb rest

Right thumb support

> ### TIP
>
> *You'll know that you have adjusted the neckstrap properly if you can put the mouthpiece into your mouth without having to bend your head up or down.*
>
> *If the mouthpiece is too far away, shorten the sling – if the mouthpiece is too close, lengthen the sling.*

Cleaning Your Saxophone

Before you put your instrument away at the end of a practice session, take a few minutes to clean it, both inside and out.

◀ Use a soft, dry cloth to clean the body of your saxophone.

It is also highly recommended that you purchase a 'pad-saver' (above right). This is made of absorbent material with a rigid wire at its core which is the same length as the saxophone. It is pushed into the instrument and stays there when the saxophone is not in use, soaking up any remaining moisture. This will prolong your saxophone's life and help to retain its value.

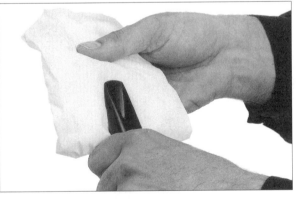

◀ Remove the mouthpiece from the neck and wipe it dry with a small cloth used only for this purpose. The reed should be dried and stored immediately.

Crook swab

▶ Use the crook swab to carefully clean inside the crook and the pull-through swab to clean the inside of the instrument body.

You can now assemble, dismantle, clean and maintain your saxophone!

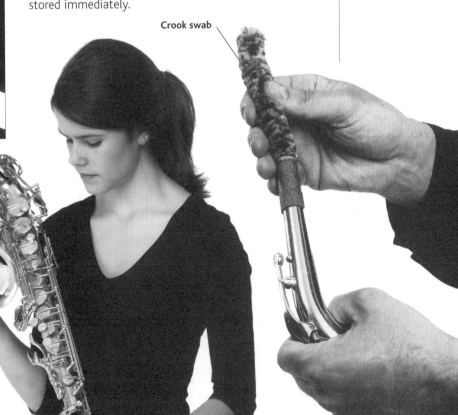

Pull-through swab

Your First Sound

IF YOU JUST can't wait another minute to hear your new saxophone, now is a good time to try to make a sound! Soon you'll be able to refine that sound, once you've learned about breathing technique and mouth position.

Don't worry about pressing down any keys to produce your first sound – just support the instrument as shown in the photograph.

1. Draw your lower lip inwards over your bottom teeth.

2. Place a quarter of the mouthpiece (reed downwards) on the lower lip.

3. Rest your upper front teeth firmly on top of the mouthpiece. Don't bite your lower lip and don't raise your head.

4. Place your tongue on the reed tip.

5. Keep your shoulders low and inhale deeply through the corners of your mouth.

6. Gently but firmly close your lips around the mouthpiece to prevent air escaping from your mouth.

7. Now say '**Tu**' as you blow through the sax.

Well done! You have produced your first sound.

Don't worry if it didn't sound quite like you had hoped – try it again after you have finished this section of the book, and you will notice an improvement.

Breathing

WITHOUT A good supply of air, your brain won't function, your hands and fingers won't move properly, and – most importantly – your saxophone won't work!

Correct breathing technique is essential in order to play the saxophone. Saxophonists – and indeed, all players of woodwind and brass instruments – must learn to breathe in a specific way in order to master their instruments.

Using Your Diaphragm

To breathe properly you need to involve your *diaphragm*. The diaphragm is the long flat muscle situated at the bottom of your lungs.

The easiest way to make yourself conscious of it is to cough. You will feel a ripple of muscle across your stomach – that's your diaphragm.

To play the saxophone, you need to aim for a prolonged contraction of the diaphragm, like a sustained cough.

This will enable you to create a controlled column of air passing from your lungs into the saxophone.

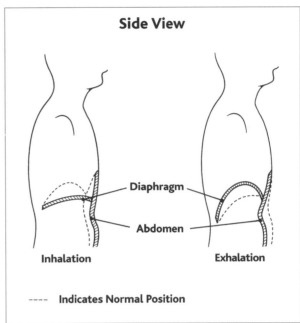

Side View

Diaphragm

Abdomen

Inhalation

Exhalation

- - - - Indicates Normal Position

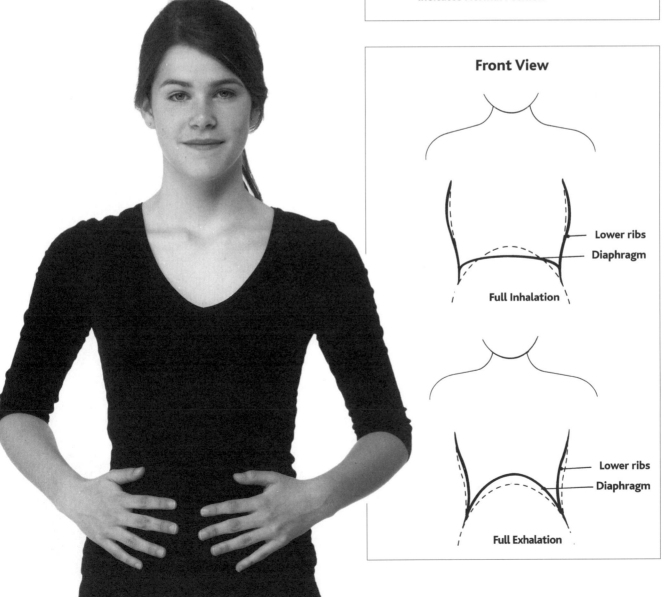

Front View

Lower ribs

Diaphragm

Full Inhalation

Lower ribs

Diaphragm

Full Exhalation

13

Practising in a standing position will help you to breathe properly. Always breathe from deep down in your stomach – not just from your chest.

Strengthening Your Diaphragm

Follow these steps to increase the strength of your diaphragm:

1. Pull your stomach muscles in slightly.

2. Push all of the air out of your lungs.

3. Close your mouth, and take in the deepest breath you can through your nose – do this as slowly as you can. Count while you are inhaling, so you know exactly how many seconds it took.

4. Hold that breath for the same number of seconds it took you to inhale.

5. Now, breathe out through your mouth, making sure that your exhalation takes exactly the same amount of time as your inhalation.

6. Repeat this exercise.

You now have a good understanding of the breathing technique needed to play the saxophone.

The saxophone needs a constant supply of air to make it work, so it is essential that you train yourself to breathe properly.

Correct use of the diaphragm allows us to take in and control more air than we would normally use.

It is impossible to produce a full tone without good support from the diapraghm – your diapraghm is also your volume control, so the louder you play the more air you will need.

Revisit this section of the book occasionally –
just like playing an instrument, good breathing takes practice!

TIP

Proper breathing requires proper posture!

Never 'slouch' while playing – make sure that you are standing straight and tall, with your shoulders back and relaxed and your feet firmly on the floor.

Practise standing firmly against a wall to get a feel for the correct playing posture.

Embouchure

THE MOUTH POSITION for playing the saxophone (or any other woodwind or brass instrument) is called the **embouchure** (pronounced *'AHM-bah-shur'*).

Follow these steps to ensure that your embouchure is correct:

1. Draw your lips gently over your teeth to prevent your front teeth from touching the reed or mouthpiece.

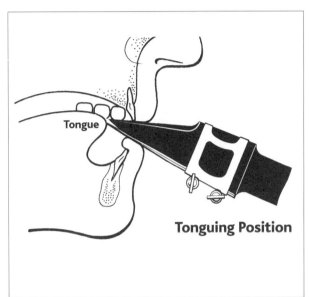

2. Keep your head up and bring the mouthpiece to your mouth. Rest the reed and mouthpiece very gently on your bottom lip.

3. Slowly push the mouthpiece into your mouth in such a way that it drags a bit of your lower lip over your bottom teeth.

Support the mouthpiece and reed with your lower lip muscles, not your teeth. The lower lip muscles should continue to cushion the reed at all times.

4. Gently, but firmly, close your lips around the mouthpiece so as to stop any air escaping.

5. Inhale, place your tongue tip gently on the reed and 'push' with your diaphragm. As soon as you feel the air pressure in your mouth, release your tongue, saying 'Tu'. **This is called 'tonguing', and this is how you stop and start the sound on a saxophone.**

TONGUING AND SOUND PRODUCTION

The tongue is to a saxophonist what the plectrum is to a guitarist – it starts the notes and ends the notes, and plays an important role in phrasing and articulation.

The release of the tongue from the reed allows a current of air to flow through the mouthpiece, causing the reed to vibrate. This vibration makes the whole sax vibrate, producing a sound.

The vibrations vary according to which keys are being pressed, and this is how the keys determine the note that you are playing.

Finger Positions

HAVE A LOOK at the pull-out chart included with this book and compare it with your instrument, trying to find all of the numbered keys.

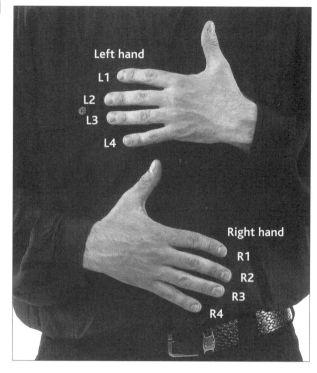

Each finger will be used to press a particular key, and each finger has a number.

The forefinger of your left hand is **L1**, and the forefinger of your right hand is **R1**.

The middle fingers are **L2** and **R2**, and so on.

Now, hook your sax back onto the sling.

Right Hand

Put your right-hand thumb under the thumb support and curl your hand around the instrument.

Place fingers R1, R2 and R3 just over the pearl finger cushions 1, 2 and 3, as shown (left).

Left Hand

Now, rest your left thumb on the thumb rest and curve your left hand around the saxophone. Let fingers L1, L2 and L3 rest above the left-hand keys 1, 2 and 3.

Take a moment to get used to these finger positions by trying this exercise – keep the mouthpiece in your mouth but don't play any notes:

1. Starting with finger L1, press and hold down one key after another – L1, L2, L3, then R1, R2 and R3.

2. Make sure that as each key is pressed none of the previous keys have been released.

3. When all six fingers are holding down their keys, start to release them one by one in reverse order.

Your First Note

NOW YOU'RE READY to put together everything you have learned about breathing, embouchure and tonguing, and play your first note.

Start with finger L1 resting above its key, and then go through the following steps:

1. Check mouth position

2. Take a deep breath

3. Place tongue tip gently on the reed

4. Press the key down

5. Push from your diaphragm to begin to exhale

6. Release your tongue

You've just played the note **B**. Hold this note for as long as your breath will allow.

Then, without disturbing the position of the mouthpiece, take a new breath either through your nose or the sides of your mouth and continue to play the note.

Make sure you don't let your lungs get empty before you take another breath.

Listen to **Track 2** to hear how the note should sound.

> ### TIP
> ●
>
> *When you take a breath, your stomach should not bulge and your shoulders should not rise.*
>
> *You should feel your back and sides expand just above your waist.*
>
> *This is how you'll know that your diaphragm is working.*

Tuning & Transposition

ON TRACK 1 of CD ONE, you will hear a tuning note that you can use at the beginning of a session, or anytime you want to check your tuning.

This note is an **A** (the customary tuning note for all instruments) but to sound this note you need to play an F♯ – this is because the alto saxophone is a transposing instrument.

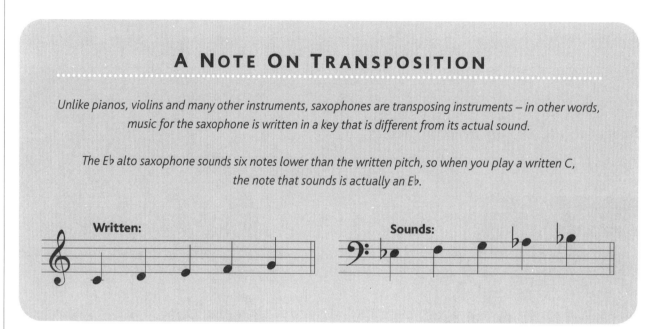

A NOTE ON TRANSPOSITION

Unlike pianos, violins and many other instruments, saxophones are transposing instruments – in other words, music for the saxophone is written in a key that is different from its actual sound.

The E♭ alto saxophone sounds six notes lower than the written pitch, so when you play a written C, the note that sounds is actually an E♭.

Written:

Sounds:

How To Tune Your Saxophone

The saxophone is tuned by changing the position of the mouthpiece on the cork of the crook.

Pushing the mouthpiece in makes the pitch sharper (higher) – pulling it out makes the pitch flatter (lower).

So if the note you are producing sounds a bit too high, pull the mouthpiece out slightly, using a gentle twisting motion. If the note you are producing sounds a bit low, push it in slightly.

Now you are ready to learn how to read and play music on your saxophone!

Your embouchure affects your intonation. By relaxing or tightening the lower jaw slightly, you will notice a slight variation in pitch – relaxing the jaw lowers the note, and tightening it raises the note.

WHAT YOU'VE LEARNED SO FAR

- How to assemble, dismantle, clean and maintain your saxophone

- Correct breathing technique, embouchure and finger positions

- Stopping and starting a note with the tongue

- How to tune your saxophone

How To Read Music

WRITTEN MUSIC has just two variables: **pitch** and **rhythm**. Pitch describes how high or low a note is, while rhythm refers to the duration of the note. An understanding of these two aspects of music will enable you to read any music for any instrument.

We have already encountered the note **B** (the first note you played). This is how the note B is written.

The stave (or staff)

As you can see, music is written on a series of five lines. These five lines are called the **stave** (or staff).

The first step towards understanding written music is being able to identify which notes are which. To do this, you need to know the name of each line and each space.

The clef

Music for the saxophone is written in the **treble clef**. The treble clef sits at the left of the stave, with one 'tail' curved around the line G.

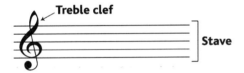

Note position on the stave

Each note is named after the line or space on which it falls.

Bars and bar lines

To make the music easier to read, the stave is divided into **bars** – the dividers are called **bar lines**. At the end of a piece or section of music, you will find a double bar line, which is like a musical 'full stop'.

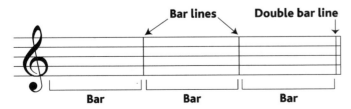

Now you know the basics of reading music!

Notes that sit just above or below a line on the stave (like the low D and the high G in the example on the left) are considered to be in a space.

In this book, you will learn several notes that are too high or too low to be written on the stave. In this case, *leger lines* are used – these extend the range of the stave to accomodate higher and lower notes.

The Note B & Your First Fingering Chart

HERE IS YOUR first note: **B**.

B

This is what the note B looks like on the fingering chart and on the stave.

L1

L2

L3

R1

R2

R3

Press down the B key as shown with finger L1 and play the note.

Listen to **Track 2** for a demonstration.

Play the note B again, but this time play 4 Bs in a row.

Here is your fingering chart for your first four notes:

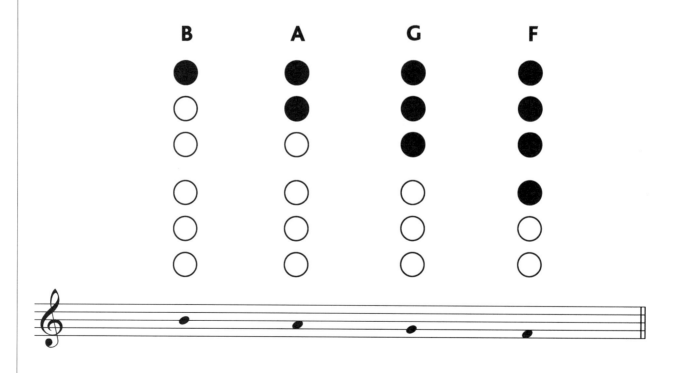

Rhythm

The beat is the rhythmic pulse that you can feel when you are listening to music. When playing you should always keep the beat by counting in your head, or tapping your foot to keep the time.

Count silently: 1, 2, 3, 4 etc.

Now, play the four Bs again, making sure that they all have exactly the same duration.

Play slowly and carefully, and always count the beat steadily – make sure you don't speed up or slow down.

Later in this book, you will learn about time signatures, which appear at the beginning of a piece of music to tell you how many beats there are in each bar.

For now, everything you play will have 4 beats per bar, so just count and play as shown, following the numbers above the stave.

Now play 8 Bs, counting in your head 1-2-3-4 before you begin.

Listen to **Track 3** for a demonstration.

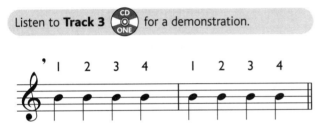

Now, you'll hold the note B for 4 counts and rest for 4 counts, then repeat according to the exercise below.

Listen to **Track 4** for a demonstration.

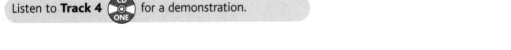

Practise this a few times, so you get used to the feeling of holding a note for 4 counts.

While you are practising this exercise, make sure that you:

- Start each note cleanly and precisely on beat 1

- Hold each note smoothly and evenly for 4 full beats

- Stop playing (rest) for the full 4 beats in each rest bar. While you are resting, relax your mouth and catch a breath

- When breathing, make sure that the position of the mouthpiece doesn't change – the mouthpiece should continue to rest on your lower lip

Play this exercise several times until you can start each note cleanly and hold it for the proper duration.

Always count a few beats in your head before starting to play so that you begin at the correct tempo.

When playing with the CD, you will always have a 'click' intro to count you in.

Your First 'Songs'

NOW YOU ARE ready to begin to play some music!

This is an excerpt from the start of the chorus of 'Yellow Submarine'. Count 4 beats per bar, and remember to tongue each note separately.

Listen to **Track 5** for a demonstration.

Yellow Submarine (excerpt)

Words & Music by John Lennon & Paul McCartney

© Copyright 1966 Northern Songs. All Rights Reserved. International Copyright Secured.

Play the notes evenly so that they all sound the same.

	1	2	3	4	, 1	2	3	4	1	2	3	4

We   all   live   in   (a yellow submarine)

The first two bars of 'Jingle Bells' are good practice for breathing, as you will have to take a very quick breath at the end of the first bar. Make sure you are holding the note on the word 'bells' for its full duration (2 counts).

Listen to **Track 6** for a demonstration.

Jingle Bells (excerpt)

Words & Music by J.S. Pierpont

© Copyright 2006 Dorsey Brothers Music Limited. All Rights Reserved. International Copyright Secured.

	, 1	2	3	4	, 1	2	3	4

Jin - gle bells   jin - gle bells

This sign ⁹ is called a 'breath mark'. It tells you where to breathe and helps you to ration your air supply accordingly. Always look over the music before playing to see where the breath marks are positioned.

Eventually you should be able to play the next example, from the Elvis classic 'Love Me Tender', in one breath.

But for now, practise taking a quick breath at the end of bar 2, hitting the first note in bar 3 precisely on the first beat.

Listen to **Track 7** for a demonstration.

Love Me Tender (excerpt)

Words & Music by Elvis Presley & Vera Matson

> Never let your breathing interfere with your embouchure. Breathe through the side of your mouth, keeping your teeth and the mouthpiece in direct contact at all times.

The next excerpt, from 'Chopsticks', is good practice for tonguing – each note should be tongued precisely and every note should have exactly the same duration.

You'll notice that this excerpt has 3 beats in each bar – this is sometimes called 'waltz rhythm'.

To feel this rhythm, give the first beat of every bar a slight accent (in other words, make it just a bit louder than the other notes in the bar).

Listen to **Track 8** for a demonstration.

Chopsticks (excerpt)

Traditional

The Note A & Tonguing Between Different Notes

HERE IS YOUR next note: **A**.

A

L1 ●
L2 ●
L3 ○

R1 ○
R2 ○
R3 ○

A

Play the note A in the example below, remembering to:

- Count and breathe during the rest bars

- Start each note precisely on the first beat of the bar

- Make sure each note starts and ends cleanly

- Play each note with a smooth, even, round tone

Play this sequence again – try to improve your sound each time, and make sure that you are giving each note its full 4 counts.

You can hear a demonstration on **Track 9**

Play along with the CD if you want to check your counting.

Now you are ready to play some tunes that put both of the notes you have learned together.
You'll also practise your tonguing and learn about a new type of articulation – **slurs**.

Tonguing between two notes

Play the excerpt from 'Streets of London' at the top of the next page, tonguing each note.

To go from B to A, you will need to keep L1 pressed down and then press L2 as well.

If you tongue the A too soon (in other words, before you have fully pressed the key) you might get a bit of a squeak – practise moving from B to A a few times until it feels comfortable and the notes are clear.

Streets Of London (excerpt)

Words & Music by Ralph McTell

How   can   you   tell   me

Strangers In The Night (excerpt)

Words by Charles Singleton & Eddie Snyder | Music by Bert Kaempfert

Here is another excerpt using the notes A and B. Tongue each note and aim for a smooth change when moving from one note to the next.

Stran-gers   in   the   night

When moving between two notes, always make sure that the pads are completely down (or completely released) before tonguing into the new note.

Legato and slurs

So far, you have been tonguing every note you play, so that each note sounds separate from the next one.

If you didn't tongue each note, the notes wouldn't be separated in this way – instead, one note would lead into the next.

This kind of playing is called **legato** (Italian for 'smoothly') and it is the opposite of tonguing – in legato playing, one note is joined to the next. A slur is a symbol that tells you when to play legato.

Play these two excerpts again, except this time play legato into each change of note, as indicated by the slurs.

Listen to **Tracks 10** and **12** to hear the examples without slurs.

Listen to **Tracks 11** and **13** to hear the examples with slurs.

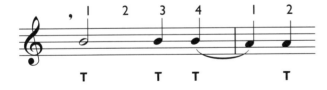

WHAT YOU'VE LEARNED IN SESSIONS 1-4

- The basics of reading music   • The notes A and B
- How to count 3 and 4 beats per bar
- How to tongue between notes
- How to observe slurs and play legato

The Note G & Note Values

HERE IS YOUR next note: **G**.

G

 L1
 L2
L3

R1
R2
R3

G

Play this short exercise to get to know your new note: **G**.

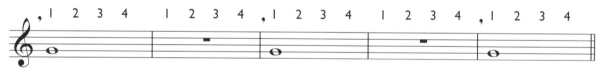

You now know the fingerings for three notes. A good way to practise them is to run through the fingerings without actually making a sound.

Without blowing, press the keys for B, then A, and then G.

Now lift them off in reverse order (remember that L1 stays down!). When you feel comfortable with the fingerings, try the next example.

Like 'Chopsticks', this example has 3 beats in each bar, and there are no slurs, so you will be tonguing each note.

Practise the fingering in bars 5 and 7 before you play, as you will be moving between B and G (skipping A) and this might take a bit of practice.

Use each bar of rest to look at the sequence of notes coming up – when you are reading music, always read ahead!

Listen to **Track 14** for a demonstration.

Note Values

By now, you will likely have realised that the amount of time given to each note – its duration – is what gives a piece of music its rhythm.

A piece can be played as fast or as slowly as you like, but the note values must be relative to each other (in other words, a note that has two counts must last exactly as long as two notes that each have one count).

In most of the pieces you have played so far, the notes have lasted one beat each.

These notes are called crotchets, or quarter notes:

This chart shows how the note values relate to each other. From the semibreve downwards, the note values are divided in half:

How to count quavers

Let's take a look at quavers, since you will soon be playing music that uses a combination of quavers and crotchets.

When quavers appear in groups of two or more, they are joined by a beam, like this:

Because quavers split the crotchet beat exactly in half, you would count them like this in a bar with four crotchet beats:

Now let's play some tunes that will help put your knowledge of notes and note values to the test.

Ob-La-Di, Ob-La-Da (excerpt)

Words & Music by John Lennon & Paul McCartney

Here is an excerpt from The Beatles' 'Ob-La-Di, Ob-La-Da', which is a four-beat bar full of quavers.

Think ahead about tonguing and the change of finger positions for the last two notes.

Listen to **Track 15** for a demonstration.

Des-mond has a bar-row in the

When you are learning a piece, start by playing very slowly – gradually increase the tempo each time you play it, always counting steadily.

Quavers and Crotchets

Practise this example to get used to combining quavers and crotchets.

Listen to **Track 16** for a demonstration.

The Lady In Red (excerpt)

Words & Music by Chris de Burgh

Here is another example of crotchets mixed with quavers.

You will no doubt recognise this tune, which is quite fast. For the purpose of this exercise you should play it as slowly as you need to in order to get it correct (by the end of this book, you'll have the opportunity – and the skills – to play the whole song up to tempo, with accompaniment!).

Count out the rhythm before you play – notice that you don't start to play until beat 4 of bar 1.

Also, watch for the short break in the music in bar 4, and make sure you come in exactly on the 'and' of beat 2.

This should give you just enough time to catch a quick breath!

If you are having trouble with this, try counting the music in bars 3 and 4 without playing, leaving a gap where the 2 should be:

1 & **2** & **3** & **4** &, **1** & _ & **3** & **4** &.

Listen to **Track 17** for a demonstration.

In the next excerpt, there are quavers, crotchets and a minim.

Watch out for

• The half-beat silence right at the beginning, which means that your first note falls on the '&' of beat 1

• The quaver that starts bar 2, and causes the minim to start on the '&' of beat 1

28

Imagine (excerpt)

Words & Music by John Lennon

Listen to **Track 18** for a demonstration.

Alouette (excerpt)

Traditional

© Copyright 2006 Dorsey Brothers Music Limited. All Rights Reserved. International Copyright Secured.

In the next tune, you will again be playing minims, crotchets and quavers. However, it's a bit less challenging since there are no 'gaps' in the rhythm.

First, play it without slurs, as shown — tongue every note, especially the quavers, cleanly and accurately.

Now play the same tune with the slurs as marked. Remember that musical phrases under slurs should be played legato, without tonguing — any notes without slurs should be tongued very clearly.

Listen to **Track 19** for a demonstration of the tune without slurs, and **Track 20** with slurs.

WHAT YOU'VE LEARNED IN SESSION 5

- Note values: crotchets, quavers, minims and semibreves
- How to move between the notes A, B and G
- How to combine note values
- How to play music that begins 'off the beat'

The Note F, Ties & Rests

NOW YOU'LL BE using your right hand for the first time, to play a new note: **F**.

F

L1 ●
L2 ●
L3 ●

R1 ●
R2 ○
R3 ○

F

Play the new note F, and then review all of the fingerings you know.

You know the notes F, G, A and B so, without playing, go from B down to F and back again several times, pressing and releasing the keys very firmly.

Then play this sequence several times:

Listen to **Track 21** for a demonstration.

Ties and Rests

Ties are very useful because they allow any number of notes of any duration to be joined together to form many interesting and varied rhythms.

A tie is a curved line that joins together notes of the same pitch, so that they are played as a continuous note. In other words, if you were to tie a minim (2 beats) to a crotchet (1 beat), the minim would be held for a total of three beats.

In this example, a G minim (2 beats) is tied to two more G minims (2 beats + 2 beats = 4 beats). So the G is played only once but is held for 6 beats.

Listen to **Track 22** for a demonstration.

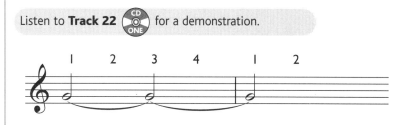

TIP

A tie looks just like a slur, but there is an easy way to tell the difference. A slur connects two or more notes of different pitch, and indicates that those notes should be played legato. A tie connects two or more notes of the same pitch, and is used to increase the duration of a note.

As long as the notes are of the same pitch, any number of notes can be tied together:

Listen to **Track 23** for a demonstration.

Strangers In The Night (excerpt)

Words by Charles Singleton & Eddie Snyder | Music by Bert Kaempfert

Track 24

You've already played a few bars of this song, but now that you've learned the note F you can play a few more! Watch out for the slur over the last phrase, and play the notes that are slurred together very smoothly ('legato').

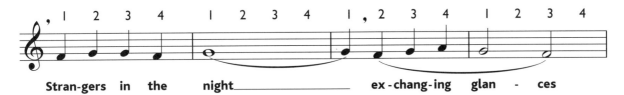

Stran-gers   in   the   night_____   ex - chang-ing   glan - ces

I Believe I Can Fly (excerpt)

Words & Music by R. Kelly

Track 25

In this excerpt, a semibreve is tied to a quaver – it might help to count the semibreve in quavers (1 & 2 & 3 & etc.).

I   be-lieve   I   can   fly,_____   I   think a-bout it   ev-'ry

Come Fly With Me (excerpt)

Words by Sammy Cahn | Music by James Van Heusen

Track 26

A few tied notes can really change the character of a tune!

Play this excerpt from 'Come Fly With Me', with the ties removed:

.....if   you   can   use some ex - o - tic   booze there's a

Now play it as it should sound, with ties extending the length of some of the quavers:

Track 27

.....if   you   can__   use__   some ex - o - tic__   booze__   there's a

Rests

Silence is just as important as sound in determining the shape and rhythm of a tune.

In some of the music that you have been playing, you have encountered signs on the stave which have required you to stop playing ('rest') for a certain number of beats. These signs are, appropriately enough, called **rests**.

The following chart shows the different types of rests and their values.

A rest is a musical sign indicating silence for a specific amount of time. Just as the note values indicate the number of beats for each note, the rest values tell you the number of beats to remain silent.

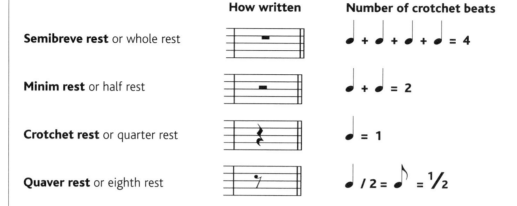

Now let's play some tunes that use rests.

Woman (excerpt)

Words & Music by John Lennon

© Copyright 1981 Lenono Music. All Rights Reserved. International Copyright Secured.

Track 28

In this excerpt, from the song 'Woman', there are 2 individual 2-beat silences written in two different ways. The first method – 2 quaver rests – is more commonly used because it helps the performer to see where the beat falls in the music.

Mamma Mia (excerpt)

Words & Music by Benny Andersson, Stig Anderson & Bjorn Ulvaeus

© Copyright 1975 Union Songs AB, Sweden. Bocu Music Limited for Great Britain and the Republic of Ireland. All Rights Reserved. International Copyright Secured.

Track 29

This excerpt, from 'Mamma Mia', has a combination of crotchet rests and quavers. For now, count in quavers. Make sure that the last quaver of each phrase ends in time for the crotchet rests get their full one-beat value.

Combining rests

If there is no note between two rests, you just add the value of the rests together.

The same applies across bar lines (as in the next excerpt) and to rests of totally different values. The key is to keep counting!

Guantanamera (excerpt)

Track 30

From time to time you will come across a rhythm that is a bit more difficult to work out.

When this happens, tapping the beat with the index finger of one hand on a surface while tapping out the rhythm of the tune with the index finger of your other hand can really help.

Try tapping the following example before you play.

Try the melody first: tap your finger when you see the symbol **V** and lift your finger when you see the symbol **∧**.

Hold your finger on the table when you see the mark ▬ .

When you are comfortable with the rhythm of the melody, tap it against a crotchet beat using your other hand.

Now try to play it!

It's very important to develop a good finger technique. Make sure that your fingers are curved at all times, and that your arms and wrists are relaxed.

Imagine (excerpt)

Track 31

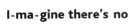

33

The Note C, Time Signatures & Dotted Notes

HERE IS YOUR next note: **C**.

C

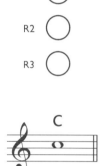

LI ○
L2 ●
L3 ○

RI ○
R2 ○
R3 ○

C

You now know the following five notes:

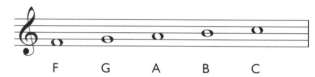

F   G   A   B   C

To remind yourself of the finger positions, finger the notes F to C and back down again several times (without blowing).

Make sure that you press and release each key very firmly, and that the pads of your fingers are right in the centre of the key pearls rather than half on or half off. Your fingers can rest on the keys but must press them only when needed.

Now play this tune to hear how C fits into the family of notes.

Listen to **Track 32** for a demonstration.

Time Signatures

From now on, you will see a time signature at the beginning of every piece you play.

If a piece has four crotchet beats in the bar the time signature will look like this:

The top number tells you how many beats are in the bar (in this case, 4), and the bottom note tells you the value of those notes.

So in $\frac{4}{4}$ time there are 4 'quarter notes' (crotchets) in a bar. $\frac{4}{4}$ is the most common time signature, and it is often written as a large **C**, as in 'common'.

The time signature $\frac{3}{4}$ means that there are 3 crotchet beats in each bar.

The time signature $\frac{2}{4}$ means that there are 2 crotchet beats in each bar.

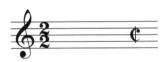

The time signature $\frac{2}{2}$ means that there are 2 minim beats in a bar.
This is sometimes called 'split' or 'cut-common' time, and sometimes 'alla breve'.

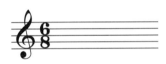

The time signature $\frac{6}{8}$ means that there are 6 quavers (eighth notes) per bar.

There are many other time signatures, and most are extensions or reductions of the ones above.

One example is $\frac{12}{8}$, which simply means there are 12 quavers in each bar.

A time signature tells you how many notes of what value fit into each bar. You will find it at the very start of a piece, just before the first note.

The top number tells you how many beats are in the bar, and the bottom number tells you the value of those notes.

Dotted Notes

You will remember that a note can be extended by tying it to another note of the same pitch.

You can also extend the duration of a note by placing a dot just to the right of it. A dot increases the value of the note by half of its original value.

In other words, a dotted crotchet lasts for 1½ beats (1 + ½) – similarly, a dotted minim lasts for 3 beats (2 + 1).

♩. = ♩ + ♪

𝅗𝅥. = 𝅗𝅥 + ♩

Any note can be extended with a dot, and the formula is always the same.

Dots can also be used with rests in exactly the same way – so a dotted minim rest would have a duration of 3 beats.

The duration of any note or rest can be extended by placing a dot after it – a dot increases the value of the note or rest by one half.

35

Tunes Using C

NOW LET'S PLAY some tunes using the note C, and incorporating the new concepts you've just learned: **dotted notes** and **time signatures**.

Before you play the next piece, look it over and notice the following:

- the time signature $\frac{3}{4}$ (3 crotchet beats in a bar)

- dotted minims (each dotted minim is 3 crotchet beats long)

- ties and slurs (ties join notes of the same pitch – slurs join notes of different pitch)

You'll notice that the numbers above the stave, which have been there to help you count have disappeared.

But don't stop counting! Always count the beats in your head.

PLAY ALONG!

From this point forward, most of the pieces you play will have an accompaniment on the CD – you can listen to a demonstration performance, then play just the backing track so you can play along.

You will always have a 'click' intro in the time signature of the piece so you'll know when to start.

Listen to **Track 33** for a demonstration – then, play along with the backing track on **Track 34**

Barcarolle from 'The Tales Of Hoffman' (excerpt)

Music by Jacques Offenbach

33 - 34

A time signature only appears at the start of a piece of music, and not at the start of each line. It stays in effect unless it is replaced by a different time signature further on in a piece.

Here is an excerpt to help you practise dotted rhythms. Remember that the dotted crotchet is worth 1½ beats.

Largo from 'New World' Symphony (excerpt)

Music by Antonin Dvořák

Track 35

Fly Me To The Moon (excerpt)

The dotted crotchet and quaver pattern create the 'lilt' that is so characteristic of a song like 'Fly Me To The Moon'.

Remember to look at the time signature and count this tune in quavers.

Fly me to the moon and let me play a-mong the (stars)

Money, Money, Money (excerpt)

36 - 37

There are no dotted notes in this piece, but you'll notice several rests which create moments of silence in the music.

Count carefully so that you are ready to come in on time – you will sometimes be starting on the second beat of a 4-beat bar.

Mo - ney mo - ney money must be fun - ny

in the rich man's world mo-ney mo-ney mo-ney

al-ways sun-ny in the rich man's world

Mo - ney mo - ney money must be fun - ny

in the rich man's world mo-ney mo-ney mo-ney

al-ways sun - ny in the rich man's world

If you have an automatic tuner, get into the habit of practising with it, especially when you are first learning to play. If you find that you are playing out of tune, listen to the pitch and adjust your embouchure and mouthpiece accordingly.

The Notes E & D And The Octave Key

HERE ARE YOUR next two notes: **E** and **D**.

E

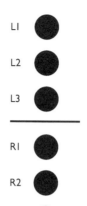

L1 ●
L2 ●
L3 ●

R1 ●
R2 ●
R3 ○

E

D

L1 ●
L2 ●
L3 ●

R1 ●
R2 ●
R3 ●

D

TIP

The notes from F downwards may be a little more difficult to start and maintain with a round tone.

To play with a better tone, relax the lower jaw a little while retaining a tight diaphragm – notes in the lower register need more breath support.

To familiarise yourself with D and E, play this tune:

Listen to **Track 38** for a demonstration.

Notes You've Learned So Far

For review, play the notes on the following chart – notice that the keys are pressed in a logical sequence as the notes get lower in pitch.

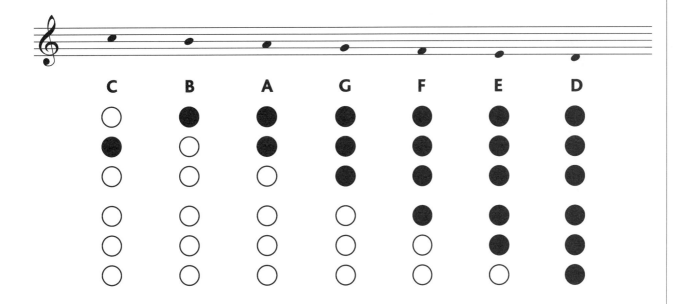

Octaves

In the chart above, picture a note on the line above the C – this note would be a new D.

Starting at the lower D, count the number of notes between it and the higher one.

You will find that there are 8 notes in total.

In other words, there is a gap, or interval, of eight notes between one D and the next D.
The musical term for this interval is an **octave**, from the word for 'eight'.

The same applies to any other note – eight notes away from C, for example, you will find another C, an octave lower or higher.

An interval is the distance between two pitches. An octave is an interval of eight notes.

39

The Octave Key

SINCE YOU CAN now play from D up to C, you just need to learn one more key in order to play the notes exactly one octave higher. This key is called the **octave key**.

The octave key is on the back of the saxophone, just above the thumb rest for your left hand (see also the pull-out fingering chart, which includes an illustration of the octave key).

The notes from your new note (D with octave key) to high C use the same pattern of fingering as in the lower register – the only difference is that you press the octave key.

Like any other key on your saxophone, the octave key must be fully depressed just before you tongue into a new note.

Now play the following example – you will hear what the octave interval sounds like for each pitch.

Track 39

The tone of each note should be as smooth and round as possible, and the crossover when opening the octave key should be noiseless.

CORRECT OCTAVE KEY TECHNIQUE

- *The thumb should at first be situated on the thumb rest, and not on the octave key, with just a small part of the end of the thumb over the octave key*

- *Press the octave key with a 'flicking' motion – in other words, the joint of the thumb (not the whole thumb) bends and presses the key*

- *Keep the thumb on the thumb rest at all times*

Here is a brief excerpt from a popular song that uses the octave key for D.

My Heart Will Go On (excerpt)

Words by Will Jennings | Music by James Horner

Near,   far,   where - ev - er   you   are____

All you have to do to play the next example is to keep holding the correct finger position for each lower note and then press the octave key for the upper note.

Play slowly, and keep the thumb on the instrument – never slide the thumb or lift it.

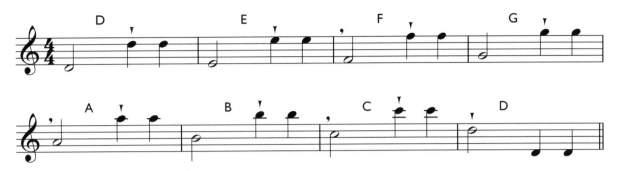

Note Pyramids

Try to play these 'note pyramids' – they are a good way to practise your octave key technique, and also your breathing and fingerings.

First, go up and down the notes without playing, just to feel the pattern of playing the keys.

Then play up the first pyramid, stopping at the breath mark. Take a comfortable breath, and continue.

Soon you will be able to play each line all the way through by taking a quick breath at the breath mark instead of stopping.

Keep in strict time within each group of eight notes – every note should be exactly the same length.

As your fingering and breathing improve, ignore the shorter slurs and play the longer ones instead – in other words, play up and down the pyramid before stopping to breathe.

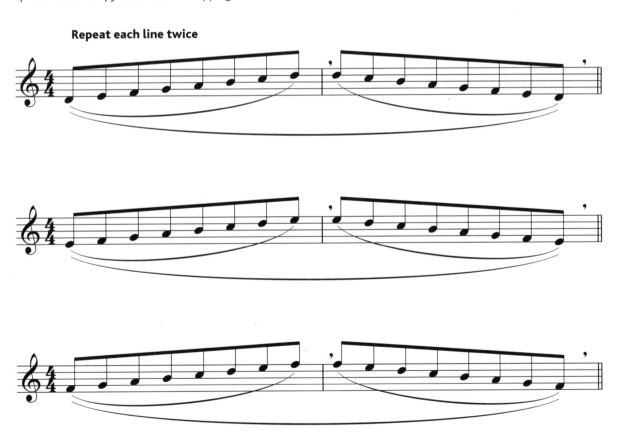

Once you have mastered these, work your way through the next 4 note pyramids: G, A, B and C.

Sharps And Flats & The Note F Sharp (G Flat)

BEFORE LEARNING your next note, F♯, you'll need to know what the sharp sign means.

The sharp sign (♯) is an **accidental** – accidentals are symbols used to raise or lower the pitch of a note.
On the stave, accidentals are placed just to the left of the note that they affect, and on the same line or space.

To raise the pitch of a note, or 'sharpen' it, you would place a sharp (♯) beside it.

To lower the pitch of a note, or 'flatten' it, you would place a flat (♭) beside it.

When you sharpen or flatten a note, it stays that way for the full bar unless you cancel it – to cancel it, you use a natural sign (♮).

Let's go back a few steps to see how accidentals work.

You know the note **F**:

You know the note **G**:

> ### ACCIDENTALS
> ··
>
> *A sharp ♯ raises the pitch of a note.*
>
> *A flat ♭ lowers the pitch of a note.*
>
> *A natural ♮ cancels the sharp or flat that has appeared before it.*

The interval (distance) between the notes F and G is one **tone**.

For example:

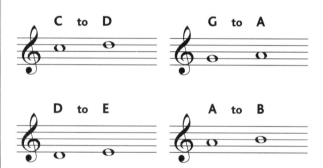

Play these intervals (including the F to G) and get used to the sound of notes that are a tone apart.

Halfway between F and G (and all the other pairs of notes above) there is another note.

The note between F and G is F sharp, and it is just a little bit higher in pitch than F – a **semitone** (or half-tone) higher, to be exact.

F-sharp can also be called G-flat – sharpening F and flattening G brings you to the very same pitch, which is (you guessed it!) right in between F and G.

Key Signatures

If, instead of making just the occasional note sharp or flat, you wanted to make a note sharp or flat for a whole piece of music, you can use a **key signature**.

For example, if the note B is to be played as B flat throughout a piece of music the key signature would look like this:

Every B, no matter how high or low, is played as B flat unless cancelled by a natural sign.

If the note F is to be F sharp throughout a piece the key signature would look like this: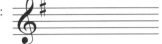

Every F, high or low, is played as F sharp unless cancelled by a natural sign.

Now you're ready to play the note F sharp (or G flat).

F♯ (G♭)

At the start of this session, you were playing one-tone intervals between several notes, including F and G. Now you can play semitone intervals too – play the following two examples to hear the difference between the intervals of a tone and a semitone.

Tones

Now play every F as an F-sharp, as indicated by the key signature:

Semitones

L1
L2
L3

R1
R2
R3

F♯/G♭

T
L1
L2
L3

R1
R2
R3

F♯/G♭

You should be starting to hear the difference between tones and semitones.

This time, you will be playing both F and F♯ in the same line. Watch out for the accidentals – you'll play F♯ in bar 1, F♮ in bar 2 and until the ♯ sign reappears.

The F♯ splits the tone between F and G, and 'leads the ear' to the G – this feeling of resolution is a distinctive feature of the semitone.

To hear this, play the next passage a few times:

You'll no doubt hear that it doesn't sound 'complete,' as a finished musical phrase would.
The reason is quite simple – the F♯ creates a tension that can be resolved only by moving to the note G:

You should hear that the note G finishes the phrase, even though the note A comes between F♯ and G.

Tears In Heaven (excerpt)

Words & Music by Eric Clapton & Will Jennings

Here is an excerpt from the song 'Tears in Heaven' to help you hear the difference between F and F♯:

I must be strong____   and car - ry on____

WHAT YOU'VE LEARNED SO FAR

• Basic principles of music notation • How to play in 4/4 and 3/4 time
• How to read key signatures and accidentals
• Intervals: tones, semitones and octaves
• How to play from D to C, including F♯, in two octaves
• Note values: semibreves, minims, crotchets and quavers
• Ties and slurs, and how to play tongued and legato passages

On the next few pages, you'll play some pieces you've already begun to learn.

Listen to the demonstration performances, and then play along with the backing tracks.

Strangers In The Night

Words by Charles Singleton & Eddie Snyder | Music by Bert Kaempfert

40 - 41

Streets of London

Words & Music by Ralph McTell

Imagine

Words & Music by John Lennon

I-ma-gine there's no hea-ven,___ it's ea-sy if you___ try;

no hell be-low us,___ a-bove us on-ly sky.

I-ma-gine all the peo-ple___ liv-ing___ for to-day.

I-ma-gine there's no coun-tries,___ it is-n't hard to___ do,

Nothing to kill or die for,___ and no re-li-gion too,

I-ma-gine all the peo-ple___ liv-ing life in peace...

You may say I'm a dream-er,___ but I'm not the on-ly one,

I hope one day you'll join us,___ and the world will live as one.

Repeat Signs & Octave Practice

HERE IS A NEW musical symbol that you will see very often – the **repeat** sign.

Repeats allow you to play full pieces of music without having to turn the page!

If the repeat sign is at the end of a piece, it means that you need to go back to beginning of the piece and repeat what you have just played.

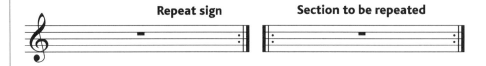

When you see two repeat signs, you simply repeat (once) all of the music between the signs.

Here is a longer excerpt from the 'New World' Symphony – you'll see that there is a section of music in the middle that you will need to repeat.

There is also an opportunity, in the last few bars, to practise moving to the higher octave.

Largo from 'New World' Symphony (excerpt)

Music by Antonin Dvořák

© Copyright 2006 Dorsey Brothers Music Limited. All Rights Reserved. International Copyright Secured.

46 - 47

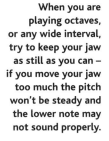

When you are playing octaves, or any wide interval, try to keep your jaw as still as you can – if you move your jaw too much the pitch won't be steady and the lower note may not sound properly.

You played a few bars of the song on the next page when you first learned about the octave key – now you can play the entire first section.

48

My Heart Will Go On (Love Theme from 'Titanic')

Words by Will Jennings | Music by James Horner

48 - 49

Ev - 'ry night in my dreams, I see you, I feel____ you,

that is how I know you go____ on.

Far a - cross the dis - tance and spa - ces be - tween____ us.

you have come to show you go____ on.

Near, far, where - ev - er you are____ I be -

- lieve that my heart will go on.____

Once more you o - pen the door____ and you're

here in my heart, and my heart will go on and____ on.

G Major Scale & First And Second Time Bars

IT'S TIME TO learn your first scale – a scale is a stepwise sequence of notes spanning an octave (and sometimes two octaves).

Play the G major scale, which looks like this:

Track 50

You'll notice that there is a sharp in the key signature – F♯. In the key of G major, F must be sharpened so that there is a semitone between F♯ and G.

The major scale is made up of a specific sequence of tones and semitones, like this:

Every major scale follows this pattern.

The next piece is a longer excerpt from 'Ob-La-Di, Ob-La-Da', in the key of G major.

To play this piece, you will need to know about first and second time bars, which go hand-in-hand with repeat signs. They look – and work – like this:

On the second time through (after you have repeated the first 3 bars), you jump from bar 3 to the second time bar.

Listen once to the demonstration track and then try to play along.

> ## TIP
> ....
>
> *Now that you've learned your first scale, you've got the perfect warm-up tool!*
>
> *Scales provide a very effective way to warm up before you play, especially if you experiment by playing them in a variety of ways.*
>
> *For example, you can play a scale in long notes to warm up your diapraghm and get the air flowing through the instrument. Or play each note several times quickly before moving on to the next note, in order to get the tongue working. Or, play the scale very slowly, then at double speed – a good way to get your fingers moving!*

Ob-La-Di, Ob-La-Da

Words & Music by John Lennon & Paul McCartney

CD ONE 51 - 52

Des-mond has a bar-row in the mar-ket place   Mol-ly is the sing-er in the

band   Des-mond says to Mol-ly, 'girl I like your   face' and Mol-ly

says this as she takes him by the hand: 'Ob-la-di____ ob-la-da____ life goes on____

____ bra,   la la how the life goes   on.   Ob-la-di

1.

____ ob-la-da____ life goes on____   bra,   la la how the life goes   on.'

2.

la la how the life goes   on.'

© Copyright 1968 Northern Songs. All Rights Reserved. International Copyright Secured.

51

When playing the scale of G major you may have noticed that the note changes of B to C and C to D are not as easy as some of the other note changes.

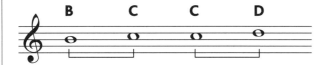

This is partly due to the design of the instrument, and also to the fact that some finger movements are more difficult than others (and therefore require more practice!).

Play the following passage until you are satisfied with the smoothness of your fingering:

Play the tune below, paying special attention to the note change from C to D.

Unchained Melody (excerpt)

Words by Hy Zaret | Music by Alex North

53 - 54

Oh,   my   love,   my   dar - ling,   I've   hun - gered   for   your

touch   a   long,   lone - ly   time._____

Time   goes   by   so   slow - ly,   and   time   can   do   so

much,   are   you   still   mine?

Practising Articulation

YOU'VE ALREADY learned the difference between legato playing and tonguing – now, here are some exercises that will help you refine both techniques.

Play these exercises slowly at first and gradually increase the speed, until you are able to slur or articulate each passage at a fairly quick tempo. These passages will help you coordinate your fingers and tongue.

Barcarolle from 'The Tales Of Hoffman' (excerpt)

CD ONE

Music by Jacques Offenbach

© Copyright 2006 Dorsey Brothers Music Limited. All Rights Reserved. International Copyright Secured.

55 - 56

Remember the 'Barcarolle' you played when you first learned about minims?

Here it is again, this time with a new articulation – the notes in each bar are slurred together.

The tongue is used to cleanly articulate those notes without a slur. All of the other notes should be played evenly, with no tongue articulation.

53

Dynamics

LISTEN TO ANY great performer and you will hear how the use of various degrees of loud and quiet playing can turn an average performance into something extraordinary. Different levels of sound – **dynamics** – are essential for a good performance.

DYNAMICS

Dynamic markings are instructions that tell the performer how loudly or quietly to play.
Dynamics are indicated by Italian words and their abbreviations – common dynamic markings include:

Fortissimo	**Very loud**	*ff*
Forte	**Loud**	*f*
Mezzo-forte	**Medium-loud**	*mf*
Mezzo-piano	**Medium-soft**	*mp*
Piano	**Soft**	*p*
Pianissimo	**Very soft**	*pp*

When dynamics are indicated in a piece of music, you might also see the following signs:

Decrescendo ▷ which means 'gradually get quieter'

Crescendo ◁ which means 'gradually get louder'

Play these examples, and observe the dynamic indications.

Track 57

William Tell Overture (Finale)

Music by Gioacchino Rossini

58 - 59

Moderate march tempo

SESSION
14

Low C And A New Time Signature $\left(\frac{6}{8}\right)$

FOR THE LOW C shown below, place your right-hand little finger (R4) over the key RS7 (the lower of the two keys).

Low C

When you start to play low notes, good breath support is essential.

Start at a higher note – say, G – and work downwards by step.

This way you'll be less likely to 'honk' when you are first learning to play this note!

Learning this note enables you to play a 2-octave C major scale, which is written like this:

Come Fly With Me (excerpt)

CD ONE

Words by Sammy Cahn | Music by James Van Heusen

60 - 61

On your CD, this song begins with a 4-bar instrumental introduction – listen to the demonstration once before you try to play along with the backing track.

Here is a piece of music for practising your low Cs. The slurs leading into the low Cs will help you to produce a full, clear sound. It continues on the top of the next page.

1. Come   fly with me,__ let's fly,___ let's fly___ a - way.___   If
(2.) fly with me,__ let's float__ down to___ Pe - ru.____   In

you can   use__ some ex - o - tic   booze__ there's a   bar   in   far Bom - bay.   Come
lla - ma   land__ there's a   one - man   band__ and he'll   toot   his   flute for   you.   Come

fly with me,___ let's fly let's fly___ a - way.___ 2. Come

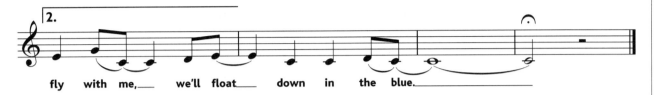

fly with me,___ we'll float___ down in the blue.___

In Session 7 you were introduced to time signatures. You've now played music written in most of the common ones, with the exception of 6/8 time.

In the excerpt below from 'Morning Has Broken', which is in 6/8 time, you will notice that each bar appears to be divided into two halves.

This is because music written in this time signature has a two-beat pulse structure. In other words, instead of the 4 pulses in a 4/4 bar, the 6/8 bar has two pulses – each of these pulses is further divided into three.

A bar of 4/4 contains 8 quavers grouped like this:

A bar of 6/8 contains 6 quavers grouped like this:

The quavers in the 4/4 example above are derived from four pulses:

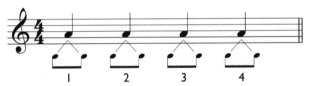

The quavers in the 6/8 example above are derived from two pulses:

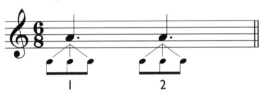

If you are having trouble playing low notes, it might help if you think of aiming your airflow toward the bottom (reed side) of the mouthpiece.

Also, make sure that your embouchure is relaxed and that your jaw is as still as possible.

Morning Has Broken (excerpt)

Words by Eleanor Farjeon | Arranged by Cat Stevens

CD ONE

62 - 63

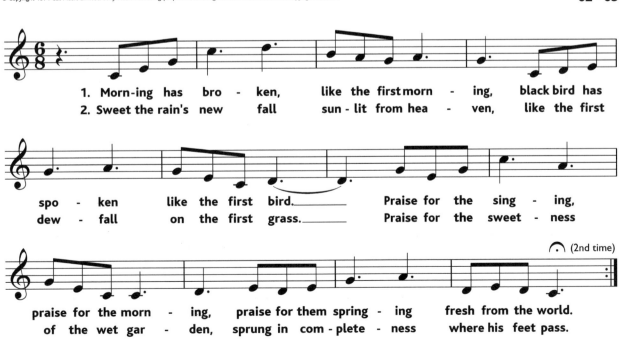

1. Morn-ing has bro - ken, like the first morn - ing, black bird has
2. Sweet the rain's new fall sun - lit from hea - ven, like the first

spo - ken like the first bird.___ Praise for the sing - ing,
dew - fall on the first grass.___ Praise for the sweet - ness

(2nd time)

praise for the morn - ing, praise for them spring - ing fresh from the world.
of the wet gar - den, sprung in com - plete - ness where his feet pass.

Practising Rhythm

YOU'VE PROBABLY noticed that your ability to read challenging rhythms is developing – however, now would be a good time to put your knowledge of rhythms to the test!

Put down your saxophone for a few minutes and clap the following rhythms:

Before you try to play a new piece, clap out the rhythm a few times – this is a great way to work out a rhythm before you start to play, and you'll find that it will make learning a new piece much easier.

New Notes B♭ And E♭ & Two New Scales

HERE ARE your next two notes:

B♭

E♭

You should also learn this alternate fingering for B♭:

L1
BIS

L2

L3

R1

R2

R3

Remember:

Just add the octave key to play the same notes one octave higher

Learning these two notes expands your knowledge of scales to include two new major scales: F major and B♭ major. Practise the scales ascending and descending, and remember to use the octave key for the high B♭ and E♭.

Scale of F major

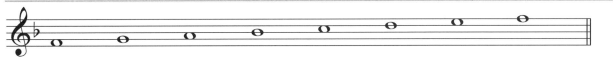

Scale of B♭ major

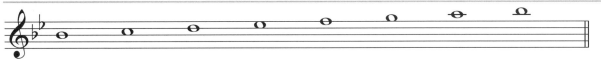

On the next pages you'll find a piece in each of these two new keys – 'Bridge Over Troubled Water' in F major, and 'Jupiter' in B♭ major.

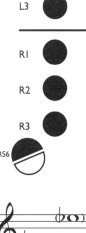

Bridge Over Troubled Water

Words & Music by Paul Simon

CD ONE

64 - 65

When you're wea - ry,___ feel - ing___ small,

when tears are in your eyes___ I'll dry them___ all.___

___ I'm on your side,___ oh,_____ when times_ get

rough___ and friends just can't be found,___ like a

bridge ov - er trou - bled wa - ter, I will lay me down. Like a

bridge ov - er trou - bled wa - ter I will lay me down.

Jupiter from 'The Planets'

Music by Gustav Holst

Andante maestoso

Codas

YOU ALREADY know about repeats and 'first and second time bars'. These symbols help you get around a piece of music, and there are a few other similar concepts you should know about.

You will often see the letters D.C. and D.S. within a song.

D.C. (from the Italian 'da capo') tells you to return to the beginning ('top') of the song.

After these letters, you will see the words 'al coda', meaning, go to the coda. A coda is the end section of a song, and it is usually very short.

Here is a diagram that represents **D.C. al Coda**.

You may also encounter the instruction 'D.S. al Fine'. This means that you jump back to the sign 𝄋 and play until you come to the word 'Fine', which means 'End'. There is an example of D.S. al Fine on page 70, in the song 'Tears From Heaven'.

If this were a piece of music, you would play bars 1, 2 and 3, then return to bar 1 and play until you get to the sign ⊕, and then jump to the coda.

D.S. (from the Italian 'dal segno') means you need to return to the sign 𝄋. In the diagram below of **D.S. al Coda**, you would play bars 1, 2 and 3, then return to bar 2, and jump to the Coda at the sign ⊕.

The next song is an example of D.C. al Coda. Look it over before you play, so you know where to go!

(Sittin' On) The Dock Of The Bay

Words & Music by Steve Cropper & Otis Redding

68 - 69

This song can be used to test your rhythmic skills! Try this – on each of the three verses, alter the rhythm of the tune to match the lyrics.

Triplets

FOR VARIETY OF rhythm, it is common to write three quavers in the time normally taken to play two. This is called a **quaver triplet**.

In a 6/8 bar, there are two main pulses divided into three 'sub pulses' (three quavers).

A bar of 6/8 contains 6 quavers grouped like this:

The quavers in the example above are derived from these pulses:

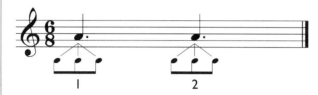

In music written in 4/4 or 2/4 time, the underlying pulse structure is 2 quavers for each crotchet.

The most common subdivision of the crotchet pulse is this:

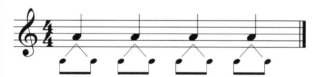

But we can also divide each crotchet into quaver triplets, like this:

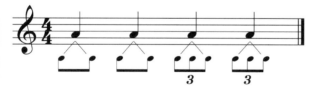

The crotchet is divided into three equal parts.

On the next page, you will find two versions of the familiar song 'Amazing Grace'. In the second version, the melody is altered through the use of quaver triplets.

Play both examples – this will give you a good understanding of how quaver triplets fit into a crotchet beat.

Amazing Grace (excerpt)

Traditional

© Copyright 2006 Dorsey Brothers Music Limited. All Rights Reserved. International Copyright Secured.

Track 70

A - maz - ing___ grace, how sweet the sound, that

saved a___ wretch like me.___ I

once was___ lost but now I'm found, was

blind but___ now I see.___

Quaver triplets

Track 71

A - maz - ing___ grace, how sweet the sound, that___

saved a wretch like___ me. I

once was___ lost but now I'm___ found_ was

blind but___ now I___ see.___

Play along to **Track 72**

Crotchet Triplets

There is another kind of triplet that you will see quite often – a **crotchet triplet**.

A crotchet triplet works very much like a quaver triplet. Just as a quaver triplet is equal to a crotchet (divided into three equal parts), a crotchet triplet is equal to a minim (divided into three equal parts).

Here is a well-known example that makes use of crotchet triplets – the theme from 'EastEnders'.

EastEnders

Music by Leslie Osborne & Simon May

CD ONE

73 - 74

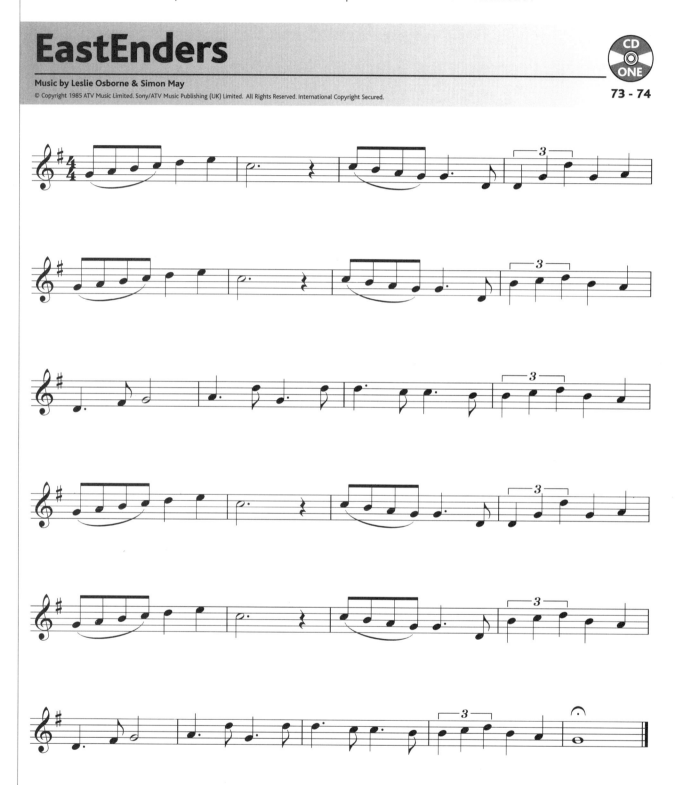

Changing Time Signatures

YOU WILL OFTEN encounter music that uses more than one time signature.

Always look a new piece over carefully so you can prepare in advance for a change of pulse.

Try the following excerpt from 'The Sound Of Silence', which moves from 4/4 time to 2/4 time and back again – count carefully during the 2/4 bars.

The Sound Of Silence

Words & Music by Paul Simon

CD TWO

1 - 2

Hel - lo dark-ness my old friend,   I've come to talk with you a - gain,

be-cause a vi-sion soft-ly creep - ing   left its seeds while I was sleep - ing,

and the   vi - sion   that was plant - ed in my   brain   still re -

mains   with-in the sound   of   si - lence

New Notes & Scales

Your next three notes are C#, low C# and G#.

C#

C#/Db

Add the octave key and you will get the C an octave higher:

C#/Db

Low C#

To play a C# an octave lower, there are substantially more fingers involved!

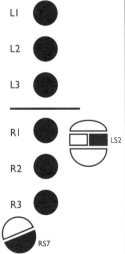

LS2

RS7

C#/Db

Now that you've learned the note C♯, you can play a D major scale.

Before you play, get used to the fingering by running up and down the scale a few times with just your fingers (ie. without blowing into the saxophone).

Your next note is G♯, also written as A♭. Learning this note will allow you to play 2 more scales: A major and E♭ major.

The note G♯ (A♭) is written and fingered like this:

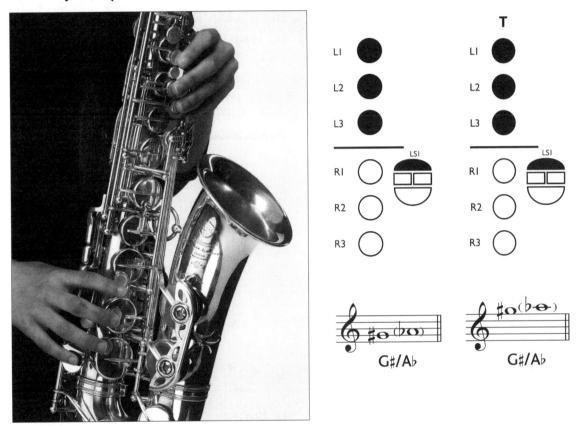

Here is the scale of E♭ Major:

And here is the scale of A Major:

On the next page you'll find a song in A Major so that you can practise playing in one of your new keys.

Tears In Heaven

Words & Music by Eric Clapton & Will Jennings

Would you know   my name

if I   saw you in hea - ven?   Will it be   the same

if I   saw you in hea - ven?   I must be strong

and car - ry on,___   'cause I   know___   I   don't be - long___   here in hea-

Fine

- ven.

Time can bring you down,___   time can bend your knee.___

Time can break your heart___ have you beg - ging please,   beg - ging please___   *(instrumental solo begins)*

Be - yond the door,___   there's peace I'm sure,___   and   I   know___

D.S. al Fine

___ there'll be   no more___   tears in hea - ven.___

Scale Review

WITH THE NOTES you have learned so far, you can play the following major scales:

C Major

G Major

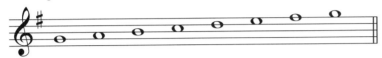

D Major

A Major

E Major

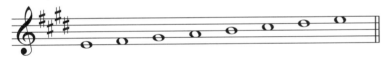

F Major

B♭ Major

E♭ Major

A♭ Major

Review these scales on a regular basis, and use them to practise your tone, articulation and finger dexterity.

Practise the scales ascending and descending – play all of the notes from the bottom to the top, and then play all the notes from the top to the bottom, without stopping.

Challenge yourself to play two octaves instead of one whenever possible.

Swing Rhythm

YOU'LL OFTEN encounter music in a swing rhythm – to give a piece of music a swing feel, you simply need to turn the written rhythm into a triplet, like this:

On **Track 5** you will hear an excerpt of the well-known swing tune 'Moonglow' as written below.

On **Track 6** you will hear it as it should be played, with a swing feel.

Listen to both versions, and then try it yourself. In a few more sessions, you'll be able to play the whole song, so make sure you are comfortable with this excerpt – and with swing rhythm – before you go further.

Moonglow (excerpt)

Words & Music by Will Hudson, Eddie De Lange & Irving Mills

5 - 6

TEMPO MARKINGS

Just like dynamics, variations in tempo can make the difference between a good and a great performance. Watch for tempo indications in every piece of music you play, as well as markings that instruct you to speed up or slow down.

Some of the most common tempo indications are as follows:

Accelerando – speeding up

Allegro – fast

Andante – slow (at a walking pace)

A tempo – at the original speed

Largo – very slow

Moderato – at a moderate tempo

Presto – very fast

Ritardando (or Rallentando) – slowing down

Staccato

WHEN YOU SEE dots above or below the heads of the notes on the stave, this indicates that you should play **staccato**. Staccato is the *opposite* of legato – notes marked staccato are to be played very detached.

Regulating the motion of the tongue with precision is the key to good staccato playing.

The correct tonguing procedure for staccato playing requires independent control of the front portion of the tongue. To practise staccato playing, tongue 'Ta-Ta-Ta' using short strokes, without changing the position of the rest of the embouchure.

The sign for a staccato note is a dot placed just above the notehead, or below it when the stems are pointing upward. This dot has the effect of approximately halving the length of the written note.

So, a dot placed under a crotchet would turn it into a quaver. Likewise, a dot placed under a quaver would shorten it to a semiquaver.

Practise these examples until you can make every note exactly the same length.

On **Track 7** (CD TWO) you will hear four quavers played legato and then again played staccato.

TIP

It's important to make sure that your reed is creating a seal with the mouthpiece, so that no air is leaking out of the sides (a common cause of 'squeaking', especially when playing short notes).

You can test the seal by covering the bottom hole of the mouthpiece tightly with the palm of your hand and 'sucking' the air out of the mouthpiece. This will make the reed seal tight against the mouthpiece. When you release your mouth, you should hear a 'pop' – this indicates that the reed is sealing properly.

If you don't hear a pop, you might want to replace your reed, and check for any cracks in the mouthpiece.

Semiquavers & Dotted Rhythms

NOW IT'S TIME to learn a new note value – the **semiquaver** – and some new dotted rhythms.

A quaver (eighth note) can be subdivided into two semiquavers (sixteenth notes):

Two quavers, then, are the equivalent of four semiquavers – both have the same duration as a crotchet (quarter note):

A dotted quaver is equal to half as much again – in other words, a dotted quaver has the same duration as three semiquavers (you'll recall that a dot after a note increases its value by one half, so a dotted quaver equals a quaver and a half, whch equals three semiquavers):

1 dotted quaver (eighth note) **3 semiquavers** (sixteenth notes)

A dotted quaver is often joined to a semiquaver with a beam, like this:

dotted quaver   **semiquaver**

Together, these two notes are equivalent to four semiquavers, or one crotchet (quarter note):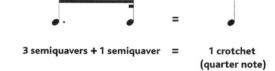

3 semiquavers + 1 semiquaver = 1 crotchet (quarter note)

The dotted quaver-semiquaver pattern has a 'lilting' rhythm:

On Track 8 you will hear eight semiquavers followed by the dotted quaver-semiquaver pattern.

Track 8 (CD TWO)

If you say the words 'humpty dumpty' a few times in a row, you will have an idea of how this would sound: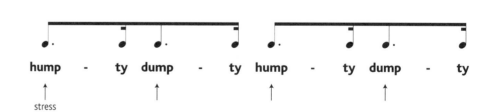

hump - ty dump - ty hump - ty dump - ty

stress

On the next page you'll find a classic example of the dotted quaver-semiquaver pattern.

Clap through the rhythm first to make sure you've got it right – then listen to the demonstration track and when you're ready, play along with the backing track.

Take The 'A' Train

Words & Music by Billy Strayhorn

You must take the 'A' train,

to go to Su-gar Hill way up in Har-lem.

If you miss the 'A' train,

you'll find you missed the quick-est way to Har-lem.

Hur-ry, get on now it's com-ing.

Lis-ten to these rails a - hum-ming. *(All aboard!)*

Get on the 'A' train,

soon you will be on Su-gar Hill in Har-lem.

Palm Keys

THE PALM KEYS allow you play the highest notes of the instrument –
you will probably have experimented with these keys already!

D

T
LI
LP3
L2
L3
R1
R2
R3

D

It's very important to stay relaxed when playing
in the high register.

The tone will only sound rich
and full if your embouchure and
fingers are as relaxed as possible,
giving the instrument the full
potential to vibrate.

Check the key diagram on the
pull-out chart if you are unsure
of any of the fingerings.

When playing these notes,
it might help to drop the left hand
slightly, lowering it gently onto
the keys, and allowing the wrist
to 'break' slightly.

The tune on the next page is
good practice for playing in the
high register.

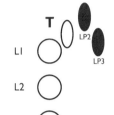

T
LP2
LI
LP3
L2
L3
R1
R2
RS1
R3

E

E♭

T
LP2
LI
LP3
L2
L3
R1
R2
R3

Eb/D#

E

A Whiter Shade Of Pale

Words by Keith Reid | Music by Gary Brooker

We skipped a light fan-dan-go___ and turned cart-wheels 'cross the floor___

I was feel-ing kind of sea-sick___ but the crowd called out for more.___

___ The room was hum-ming hard-er___ as the ceil-ing flew a-way___

when we called out for an-oth-er drink,___ the wait-er brought a tray. And so it

was___ that la-ter as the mil-ler told his tale___

that her face at first just ghostly turned a whi-ter___ shade of pale.___

ritardando

Vibrato

VIBRATO IS defined as the controlled fluctuation of pitch, and it can bring a whole new dimension to your playing.

The benefits of using vibrato include:

• Improved tone quality

• Better pitch control

• Expressivity

Follow these two steps to play vibrato:

1. Play a middle-range note (A, B or C). While you are playing the note, drop the jaw slightly – you should feel as if you are saying 'wah' into the saxophone.

2. Raise the jaw back to its original level, saying 'ooh'.

Note that when you dropped your jaw, the pitch was lowered slightly – when you raised your jaw, the pitch returned to where it was. These are the very simple mechanics behind vibrato technique.

Now, try it again in 4/4 time with a dotted crotchet-quaver beat – follow the diagram below:

Notice that all the notes in these exercises are tied together – sound the first note of each line and hold it while you move your jaw in time.

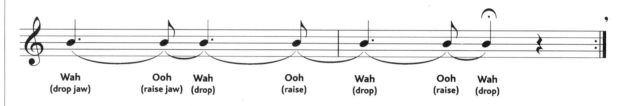

Wah	Ooh	Wah	Ooh	Wah	Ooh	Wah
(drop jaw)	(raise jaw)	(drop)	(raise)	(drop)	(raise)	(drop)

Now, try it in dotted quavers with semiquavers:

When you are practising these vibrato exercises, make sure you move your jaw very quickly from one position to the next – exaggerate the motion at first until it begins to feel natural.

Wah - Ooh   Wah - Ooh   Wah - Ooh   Wah - Ooh   Wah - Ooh   Wah - Ooh   Wah - Ooh   Wah - Ooh

Listen to **Track 13** 🔘 for demonstrations of the vibrato exercises above, followed by one held note played vibrato.

The next piece would sound lifeless were it not for the use of vibrato.

Be aware of the small notes before the note F in bar 2 – these are called **grace notes**, and they should be 'squeezed' in just before the beat.

The Old Castle from 'Pictures At An Exhibition'

Music by Modest Petrovitch Mussorgsky

Slow, with feeling

p vibrato

TIP

As you've just learned, lowering and raising the jaw while holding a note produces vibrato.
You may also have noticed that when you dropped your jaw, the sound was much fuller –
this is because lowering your jaw allows the reed to vibrate more freely.

Practise holding long tones with your jaw in a lowered position, as this is a good way to strengthen
your embouchure and improve the fullness of your sound.
If your mouth begins to feel tired, try to keep playing – this is a sign that you are
developing your embouchure muscles.

Practising Tonguing

AS YOU KNOW, the removal of the tongue from the reed is what starts a note – the start of a note is called the **attack**.

Conversely, the termination of a note is called the **release**. To release the note, or stop it from sounding, the tongue is once again applied to the reed.

Stopping a note requires just as much skill and practice as starting a note. When you are about to release (stop) a note, try to avoid a change in pitch. Also, stay in time and make sure the tone is even.

To release a note, place the tip of the tongue cleanly on the back of the reed, always ensuring that the airstream from your lungs is steady and constant.

After the attack, the tongue should remain at the bottom of the mouth cavity, close to the reed. This position will allow it to strike up and stop the sound when needed.

Work on the following tunes to refine your tonguing technique:

The Tenpenny Bit

Traditional

16 - 17

St. Patrick's Day

Traditional

18 - 19

Minor Scales

TO THIS POINT, all of the music you have played has been in major keys.
A very brief introduction to the minor keys will help you in the next piece, the theme from 'The Godfather', which is in D minor.

Minor keys are often described as 'sad-sounding' compared to major keys – they are often used for music that is more melancholy, or 'dark', in mood.

Each major scale has a 'relative' minor scale – that is, they share the same key signature. To find out which minor scale would be 'relative' to a given major key, you simply count down three semitones from the first note of the major scale:

C major: 3 semitones below C is A, so **A minor** is the relative minor key
G major: 3 semitones below G is E, so **E minor** is the relative minor key
F major: 3 semitones below F is D, so **D minor** is the relative minor key

There are different types of minor scales – melodic, harmonic, natural – but we'll focus only on the harmonic minor.

A minor scale has the same sharps and flats as its relative major scale, with one important exception – the second last note of the scale is raised by one semitone (so in D minor, which relates to F major, there is a B♭ but also a C♯):

Look at the diagram below, which compares the scales F major and D minor. Like the major scale, the minor scale is made up of a specific pattern of tones and semitones. The diagram shows the intervals that make up the scales, as a series of tones (T) and semitones (S).

Track 20

On Track 20 you will hear an F Major scale followed by a D Minor scale.

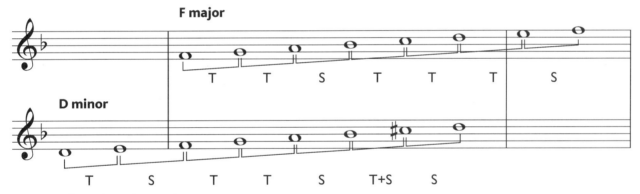

Here are a few other minor scales to try:

A Minor

E Minor

B Minor

The Godfather (Main Theme)

Words by Larry Kusik | Music by Nino Rota

Now you're ready to play some full songs!

Before you try to play the solos in the back of the book, read through the practice tips on the next page.

Practice Tips & Solos

1. Always remember the importance of tone quality. If you are not happy with your tone, ask yourself the following questions:

• Is my posture as good as it can be?

• Am I thinking about my breathing, and giving the sound the support it needs?

• Am I breathing from my diaphragm or from my chest? (If you feel that you are breathing from your chest, review the notes on diaphragmatic breathing on page 13 of this book).

2. Listen carefully to the pitch of every note you play.

To develop good intonation, align your pitch with a piano. Listen to other players and be aware of the accuracy of their pitch. Record yourself playing whenever possible – you will be surprised at how much you hear!

3. Always warm up – this will help you achieve relaxation and flexibility in both your fingers and your embouchure, and will ensure that you are blowing warm air instead of cold into the saxophone.

The scales you have learned in this book make ideal warm-up exercises – practise them first in minims (2 per bar), then in crotchets (4 per bar), and then in quavers. This is a great way to teach your fingers to move with ease.

On the next several pages you will find some complete songs to play.

There are demonstrations on the CD, and also backing tracks so you can play along.

There will always be an introduction before you come in, and this will be indicated by a number of bars of rest at the beginning of the music – count carefully so you know when to come in.

Also be aware of any periods of rest in the middle of the songs – count these out and be ready (with a good breath) to start playing when it's time.

And finally – don't forget to make music! Once you have learned a piece, remember all of the 'extras' that can make it come to life, including dynamics, articulation and vibrato.

Good luck!

Moonglow

Words & Music by Will Hudson, Eddie De Lange & Irving Mills

The Lady In Red

Words & Music by Chris de Burgh

repeat three times

Somethin' Stupid

Words & Music by C. Carson Parks

Repeat to fade

I Guess That's Why They Call It The Blues

Words & Music by Elton John, Bernie Taupin & Davey Johnstone

(harmonica solo)

solo continues

Don't Know Why

Words & Music by Jesse Harris

To Coda

2.

D.S. al Coda

⊕ Coda

rit.

Clocks

Words & Music By Guy Berryman, Chris Martin, Jon Buckland & Will Champion

(2nd time one octave higher)

Congratulations!

YOU'VE PROGRESSED from the basics of playing the alto saxophone and reading music, all the way to playing full tunes with accompaniment.

Now you're ready to take your playing to the next level – with what you have learned in this book, you should be able to handle just about any piece of music that comes your way.

The titles below will get you started.

Guest Spot

Here's your chance to become a true soloist! Step into the spotlight and play along with the superb backing tracks on the specially recorded CDs. The *Guest Spot* series includes more than 30 titles, featuring everything from classical and music theatre, to pop, rock and soul.

Guest Spot: Classical Favourites
Includes Mozart's *Musical Joke*, Schubert's *Entr'acte*, selections from Handel's *Water Music*, and more.
AM984445

Guest Spot: The Rat Pack
Includes *The Lady Is A Tramp*, *My Way*, *Ain't That A Kick In The Head*, and more.
AM983378

Guest Spot: Soul
Includes *Stand By Me*, *I Heard It Through The Grapevine*, *I Got You (I Feel Good)*, and more.
AM970211

Blues For Saxophone
Sixty-seven all-time favourite blues numbers specially arranged for E♭ and B♭ saxophones by Jack Long, complete with chord symbols in concert pitch. Includes *Basin Street Blues*, *Harlem Nocturne*, and *Straight No Chaser*.
AM952028

The Beatles For Sax
Seventy-two Beatles favourites in arrangements for saxophone. The book includes songs from across the band's highly varied career, and all are suitable for both B♭ and E♭ instruments.
NO91058

Go Solo! Improvisation For Alto Sax
Unlock the secrets of jazz-style improvisation the easy way with this informative book and CD. Whether you read from music or just play by ear, this unique tutor shows you step-by-step how to 'compose as you play'. Ten example patterns are included for each song, with tips and advice to help you develop your own ideas and licks.
AM91326